USHER

Poems

USHER

Poems

B. H. FAIRCHILD

W. W. NORTON & COMPANY

NEW YORK   LONDON

For information about permission to reproduce selections from this book,
write to Permissions, W. W. Norton & Company, Inc., 500 Fifth Avenue
New York, NY 10110

For information about special discounts for bulk purchases, please contact
W. W. Norton Special Sales at specialsales@wwnorton.com or 800-233-4830

Manufacturing by Courier Westford
Book design by Lovedog Studio
Production manager: Anna Oler

Library of Congress Cataloging-in-Publication Data

Fairchild, B.H.
Usher : poems / B. H. Fairchild. — 1st ed.
p. cm.
ISBN 978-0-393-06575-6
I. Title.
PS3556.A3625U84 2009
811'.54—dc22   2009005617

W. W. Norton & Company, Inc.
500 Fifth Avenue, New York, N.Y. 10110
www.wwnorton.com

W. W. Norton & Company Ltd.
Castle House, 75/76 Wells Street, London W1T 3QT

1 2 3 4 5 6 7 8 9 0

For three poet-teachers:

Anthony Hecht and

Winston Weathers, *in memoriam,*

and Don Welch

Contents

FIVE PROSE POEMS FROM THE JOURNALS OF
ROY ELDRIDGE GARCIA

THE BEAUTY OF ABANDONED TOWNS

DESIRE

Acknowledgments

I wish to thank the National Endowment for the Arts and the Lannan Foundation, with whose support many of these poems were written. I also want to thank family and friends for advice and discussion about certain poems and/or their subject matter: Patricia Fairchild, Paul Fairchild, Jim Bogen, Matt Davidson, Chic Goldsmid (whose wonderful store, Claremont Books and Prints, was the source for much of my reading relevant to this project), R. S. Gwynn, Wendy Herbert, H. L. Hix, Sant Khalsa, Paul Mariani, David Mason, Frances McConnell, Robert Mezey, the late D. Z. Phillips, Kurt Smith and his *Tractatus* seminar, and Dr. Richard F. Taylor. Grateful acknowledgment is also made to the following publications for poems and prose that originally appeared in them (although, in some cases, in different form).

American Literary Review: "Hume," "*Madonna and Child, Perryton, Texas, 1967*," "Wittgenstein, Dying"
Art/Life: "Night Terrors"
Columbia: "Working Men in Their Sunday Clothes"
Connecticut Review: "Bloom School," "The Teller"
Green Mountains Review: "Piano"
Hudson Review: "Gödel," "Les Passages," "Poetry Night at the Frost Place," "What He Said"

Image: "Trilogy" ("Freida Pushnik," "Usher," "Hart Crane in Havana")

New Letters: "The Cottonwood Lounge"

New South: "The Deer"

Nightsun: "Household," "Wheat"

Ploughshares: "The Beauty of Abandoned Towns"

Rivendell: "Final Exam"

Sewanee Review: "Maria," "Nathan Gold," "*On the Waterfront*"

Shenandoah: "The Barber," "Moth"

Smartish Pace: "Cendrars," "*Les Saltimbanques au repos*," "Leaving" (under the title, "Thomas McGrath")

Southern Poetry Review: "Desire"

TriQuarterly: "The Church of the New Jerusalem, Pawnee Rock, Kansas," "The Gray Man"

Trilogy was published as a limited-edition, fine press book by PennyRoyal Press in 2008, with illustrations by Barry Moser and an introduction by Paul Mariani.

USHER

Poems

I think of cinemas, panoramic sleights
With multitudes bent toward some flashing scene
Never disclosed but hastened to again,
Foretold to other eyes on the same screen . . .

—Hart Crane, "To Brooklyn Bridge"

The Gray Man

We are cutting weeds and sunflowers on the shoulder,
the gray man and I, red dust coiling up around us,
muddying our sweat-smeared mugs, clogging our hair,
the iron heel of an August Kansas sun pushing down
on the scythes we raise against it and swing down
in an almost homicidal rage and drunken weariness.
And I keep my distance. He's a new hire just off
the highway, a hitchhiker sick to death of hunger,
the cruelties of the road, and our boss hates
poverty just enough to hire it, even this old man,
a dead, leaden pall upon his skin so vile it makes you
pull away, the gray trousers and state-issue black
prison boots, the bloodless, grim, unmoving lips,
and the eyes set in concrete, dark hallways that lead
to darker rooms down somewhere in the basement
of the soul's despair. Two weeks. He hasn't said
a word. *He's a goddamned ghost,* I tell my father.
Light flashes from his scythe as he decapitates
big clumps of yellow blooms, a flailing, brutal war
against the lords of labor, I suppose, against the state,
the world, himself, who knows. When we break,
I watch the canteen's water bleed from the corners
of his mouth, a spreading wound across his shirt,
the way he spits into the swollen pile of bluestem

and rank bindweed as if he hates it and everything
that grows, a hatred that has roots and thickens,
twisting, snarled around itself. A lizard wanders
into sunlight, and he hacks at it, chopping clods
until dust clouds rise like mist around him, and then
he speaks in a kind of shattering of glass cutting
through the hot wind's sigh, the fear: *Love thine enemy.*
He says it to the weeds or maybe what they stand for.
Then, knees buckling, with a rasping, gutted sob
as if drowning in that slough of dirty air, he begins,
trembling, to cry.

          I was a boy. The plains' wind
leaned against the uncut weeds. High wires hummed
with human voices in their travail. And the highway
I had worked but never traveled lay across the fields
and vanished in that distant gray where day meets night.

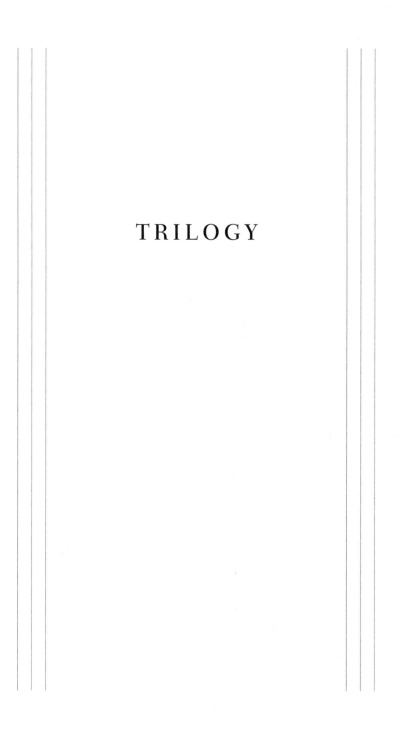

TRILOGY

Truly, thou art a God who hidest thyself.

—Isaiah 45:15

Abundant hazards,
being and non-being, every fleck through which
this time affords
unobliterate certainties | hidden in light:

—Geoffrey Hill, "Offertorium: Suffolk, July 2003"

The "meters," chandas, *are the robes that the gods "wrapped*
around themselves," acchadayan, *so that they might come*
near to the fire without being disfigured as though by the
blade of a razor.

—Robert Calasso, *Literature and the Gods,*
commenting on the *Satapatha Brahmana*

Frieda Pushnik

"Little Frieda Pushnik, the Armless, Legless Girl Wonder," who spent years as a touring attraction for Ripley's Believe It or Not and Ringling Brothers and Barnum and Bailey . . .

—"Obituaries," *Los Angeles Times*

These are the faces I love. Adrift with wonder,
big-eyed as infants and famished for that *strangeness*
in the world they haven't known since early childhood,
they are monsters of innocence who gladly shoulder
the burden of the blessed, the unbroken, the beautiful,
the lost. They should be walking on their lovely knees
like pilgrims to that shrine in Guadalupe, where
I failed to draw a crowd. I might even be their weird
little saint, though God knows *I've wanted everything
they've wanted,* and more, of course. When we toured Texas,
west from San Antonio, those tiny cow towns flung
like pearls from the broken necklace of the Rio Grande,
I looked out on a near-infinity of rangeland
and far blue mountains, avatars of emptiness,
minor gods of that vast and impossibly pure nothing
to whom I spoke my little stillborn, ritual prayer.

I'm not on those posters they paste all over town,
those silent orgies of secondary colors—jade,
burnt orange, purple—each one a shrieking anthem
to the exotic: Bengal tigers, ubiquitous
as alley cats, raw with not inhuman but
superhuman beauty, demonic spider monkeys,
absurdly buxom dancers clad in gossamer,
and spiritual gray elephants, trunks raised like arms
to Allah. Franciscan murals of plenitude,
brute vitality ripe with the fruit of eros,
the faint blush of sin, and I am not there. Rather,
my role is the unadvertised, secret, wholly
unexpected thrill you find within. A discovery.
Irresistible, like sex.

     So here I am. The crowd
leaks in—halting, unsure, a bit like mourners
at a funeral but without the grief. And there is
always something damp, interior, and, well,
sticky about them, cotton-candy souls that smear
the bad air, funky, bleak. All, quite forgettable,
except for three. A woman, middle-aged, plain
and unwrinkled as her Salvation Army uniform,
bland as oatmeal but with this heavy, leaden sorrow
pulling at her eyelids and the corners of her mouth.
Front row four times, weeping, weeping constantly,
then looking up, lips moving in a silent prayer,
I think, and blotting tears with a kind of practiced,
automatic movement somehow suggesting that
the sorrow is her own and I'm her mirror now,

the little well of suffering from which she drinks.
A minister once told me to embrace my sorrow.
To hell with that, I said, *embrace your own.* And then
there was that nice young woman, Arbus, who came and talked,
talked brilliantly, took hours setting up the shot,
then said, *I'm very sorry,* and just walked away.
The way the sunlight plunges through the opening
at the top around the center tent pole like a spotlight
cutting through the smutty air, and it fell on him,
the third, a boy of maybe sixteen, hardly grown,
sitting in the fourth row, not too far but not too close,
red hair flaring numinous, ears big as hands,
gray eyes that nailed themselves to mine. My mother,
I remember, looked at me that way. And a smile
not quite a smile. He came twice. And that second time,
just before I thanked the crowd, *I'm so glad you could
drop by, please tell your friends,* his hand rose—floated,
really—to his chest. It was a wave. The slightest,
shyest wave good-bye, hello (and what's the difference,
anyway) as if he knew me, *truly* knew me, as if,
someday, he might return. His eyes. His hair, as vivid
as the howdahs on those elephants. In the posters
where I'm not. That day the crowd seemed to slither out,
to ooze, I thought, like reptiles—sluggish, sleek, gut-hungry
for the pleasures of the world, the prize, the magic number,
the winning shot, the doll from the rifle booth, the girl
he gives it to, the snow cone dripping, the popcorn dyed
with all the colors of the rainbow, the *rainbow,* the sky
it crowns, and whatever lies beyond, the One, perhaps,

we're told, enthroned there who in love or rage or spasm
of inscrutable desire made that teeming, oozing,
devouring throng borne now into the midway's sunlight,
that vanished, forever silent God to whom I say
again my little prayer: *let me be one of them.*

Usher

*1954, Nathan Gold, a student at Union Theological
Seminary, working part-time at the Loews 83rd Street
Theater, Manhattan*

Dear Sollie,
            Master of Kaballah, each cryptic point
of David's star, now casting I-Ching hexagrams
in hipster Berkeley. So this one's in hexameters,
an undercurrent, roughly six feet under—no,
not death, but bad news, fear and failure, everywhere:
Robert Moses, goddamned Cross Bronx Expressway,
the parting of the Red Sea is what that fascist bastard
thinks, I'm betting, though the Golds were never Reds
except for Uncle Mike, and now where do they go,
exiled from their homeland and beloved Yankees.
And Sivan in her condition. And their turncoat son
leading goyim and Manhattan's great unwashed
down dark aisles to pray before the gleaming gods
of Hollywood, returning each day to the classrooms
of German theologians for whom God is a puzzle,
a conundrum made darker yet by that Danish Rabbi,
Kierkegaard. So here I wait, lean on gilded,
faux-Moroccan walls, and stare worshipfully
at plaster masks of tragedy and big-mouthed

comedy hung overhead, blue-green bulbs
for eyes that blindly gaze not at but over us,
lost in their abstractions and detached as always
from the laity, their stench and squalor, floors pocked
with Dubble Bubble and the stale, mingled smells
of soda, buttered popcorn, licorice, and ammonia.
Mr. Hinkle, our gin-head manager, has passed out
in the upstairs office once again, and Brownie,
the homunculus projectionist, is no doubt reading
fuck books and sucking Jujubes and Milk Duds
while I wait, armed with flashlight and Kierkegaard,
that monster, *Either/Or*, because my paper's overdue
(though useless, really, after yesterday's debacle).
Are those made happy by *A Star Is Born*, warmed
by love's ruin and resurrection in *The Country Girl*
really in *despair*? Churchyard, that joy killer,
thinks so. I say, let them wallow in the shallows
of the silver screen, the smart-assed repartee of Tracy
and brainy Hepburn, the lurid technicolor charms
of VistaVision, Gene Kelly dancing in the rain,
Gary Cooper's quick-draw Jesus in *High Noon*.
Tillich just won't stop with his *ultimate concern,
ground of being, courage of despair,* his *God
above God,* and in between, *illusions*: movies, yes,
but more, the life that copies them. Crossing Eighth,
I saw a woman, hair swept across one eye
like Rita Hayworth, walk into a bus-stop bench.
Blind humanity. Niebuhr would have loved it,
Tillich, too, *the grandeur and the misery,* New York,

the world, everything's a metaphor to them.
But misery like Sivan's, glioblastoma multiforme,
do they know *that,* those Graeco-Latin syllables
baroque and swollen as the thing itself, fat tumor
feeding on the brain, burning from the center
out, and those prick doctors without the balls to give
one cc more Dilaudid than the law allows.
So there I am, just another addict trafficking
in horse among the freaks of Hubert's Dime Museum
and scoring D from the trembling future surgeon
who uses it to pay tuition. God, the crap
we do to make a life. *Sin?* The *world* is sin.
We go down, oh, I mean *down,* into that basement:
Jesus, those little stages dim with burnt-out bulbs,
the curtains jerk back, lo, and there is lovely Olga
and her beard, Sealo the Seal Boy, The Armless Wonder,
Albert-Alberta in his/her hermaphroditic glory.
Baudelaire's "floating lives," or as Sivan said,
"Disneyland in hell." But, of course, they're us,
we're them, and we pay the price, cheap as it is, to see
ourselves.

       Ah, New York when she was well: Al Flosso's
magic shop on 34th, my God, late Saturday
one afternoon strolling down from Central Park,
bronze leaves spilled like coins along Eighth Avenue,
and there's Al himself pulling quarters from the ears
of little kids who spend them all on props, Zombies,
Imp Bottles, Crazy Cubes, tricks for turning water
into wine, if happiness is wine made holy,

and I think it is, or was. Later, fine dining
at the Automat to save a buck, Eucharist
at Smokey Mary's, then all those jazz clubs lining
52nd Street, and that's the night at Birdland
the great Eddie "Lockjaw" Davis went toe-to-toe
with Sonny Stitt. *Pure heaven.* Jimmy Ryan's, Five Spot,
The Famous Door, Three Deuces, Sivan's long auburn
hair now gone but brilliant then, bathed in neon,
big riffs streaming out of every door, a kind
of aural exegesis of forbidden texts:
"Love for Sale," "Strange Fruit," "Ornithology."

Long time passing. Then yesterday in systematics
Tillich demolishing Parmenides by way
of Plato's *Sophist*: *Any image is a blending*:
Nonbeing closed in Being (my loose translation).
And so the movies, the technology of film:
the image held before our flawed, half-blind gaze,
black ribs separating every frame, that darkness
never seen but always there: in *On the Waterfront*,
Saint and Brando in the fulcrum of their fates,
Manhattan floating in the thinning, pearl-gray light
behind them, and that cinematic night surrounding
every second of their ticking lives, unseen,
ubiquitous: Nonbeing, nothingness, the ontic
absence at the center, or between the frames,
of the waking life. "I could have been a contender
. . . *instead of who I am*," pleads Brando to his brother:
who he's *not* held forever in the embrace of who he *is*.

"*Persistence of vision,*" I tell Tillich, *that's what it's called,*
the fantasy of life in motion while in fact
a little death, NONBEING, *separates each frame,*
each moment in the shadow play of happiness,
and God in all His wisdom is the projectionist!
THAT'S OUR METAPHOR! *Wrong God,* he says. *The God*
that can be known cannot be God. Well, that finished it.
I swear, the man's a neo-Gnostic, a magician.
Imagine, the greatest theologian in America,
a Bronx Jew shouting at him: *THEN WHO THE FUCK*
IS GOD? So, THE END. Alpha and Omega. Sivan
said from the beginning it would end this way.

I'm an usher, Sol. That's all. Light in hand, I take
them down, or up, the Heraclitean way, into
that little night, into—no, not Plato's cave, Lascaux
or Rheims—but the purest form of K's *aesthetic* life,
and there they sit with the passivity of angels,
God's children in their ontic moment, looking on,
amused, uplifted, frightened, haunted, grieved, lost
in the deceptions of *the beautiful,* the real unreal,
and they are for those ninety stolen minutes *saved*:
Pavlic, from the corner newsstand, shutting down
for matinees—war films, westerns; Mrs. Kriegan,
who cleans bathrooms at St. Bart's and weeps through all
the love scenes; Sivan, too—turbaned, thin—at every
bargain twilight show for *Singin' in the Rain,*
she knew all the tunes and sang them sotto voce
on the subway home; that sad, small man who wore

Hawaiian ties, a Dodgers cap, and tennis shoes,
saying, every time, the rosary on his way out.
All of them, the drunks, bums, lovers, priests, housewives,
cops, street punks shooting up, whores giving blowjobs
in the balcony. I usher. I take them there.

Remember Colmar, the Isenheim, when we were high
on weed, big brass gong of the risen sun, His hands
pushing outward from within, and you, my brother,
in your reefer madness, cactus, and who knows what
shouting "Fire" till I could bring you down? Today
in *Country Girl,* Grace Kelly at the ironing board,
and Brownie upstairs falls asleep at the projector, film
sticking, flap, flap, then stuck, no one to turn the lamp off,
small ghosts of smoke, a black hole starting in the center
of the frame, (the Big Bang must have looked like that),
flame eating outward at the curling edges, spreading,
Grace swallowed slowly by the widening fire, then gone,
the film snaps, bringing down an avalanche of light,
the sun's flood a billion years from now, earth sucked
into the flames, lurid, omnivorous, the whole room
stunned and silvered with it, shadows peeled away,
each gray scarf, each shawl of darkness lifted, the audience
revealed in all their nakedness, their *uncoveredness*
and soiled humanity, among the candy wrappers,
condoms, butts, crushed Dixie cups, as we wait for Grace
to reappear, the iron to move, the mouth to speak,
for love, Sol, the movie of our lives, and for Sivan.

Hart Crane in Havana

April 26, 1932: *They breakfasted on board before*
making their way into Havana, and after Hart had
pointed out the cafe where they were to meet, . . . he
slipped down a street in the white, gold, and azure
Cuban capital and for one of the few times in his life
disappeared entirely. He wrote postcards . . .

—Clive Fisher, *Hart Crane: A Life*

And saw thee dive to kiss that destiny
Like one white meteor, sacrosanct and blent
At last with all that's consummate and free
There, where the first and last gods keep thy tent.

—*The Bridge*

Dear Wilbur,
    In Havana, Hotel Ambos Mundos,
<u>Orizaba</u> docked six hours, and I'm drinking
Sazeracs (absinthe and bourbon), <u>sans ami</u>
though recall Ramón Novarro in L.A? Second
only to the Hoover in the cupola Grace
caught me with. No adventures here, home soon
if I can face it—empty-handed, Guggenheim

33

exhausted. View from absinthe-land: blue and gold
like the Maxfield Parrish prints my father used
to decorate his candy boxes.

As ever, Hart

Dear Sambo,

Je ne suis pas Rimbaud! though once I was.
Her undinal vast belly moonward bends. Such lines
extinct now. Prescription: iodine followed by
a bottle of Mercurochrome, slashing Siqueiros's
portrait with a razor blade. When Lawrence talks of
"going down to the dark gods," he means sex of course
rather than its sister, death. Remember Hartley's tale
of Albert Ryder, standing just outside his hostess's
window watching Christmas dinner? Thank you so much
for inviting me. A freak, Sam, is what I am. So praise
to you and Otto Kahn,

the uninvited heart

Dear Bill,

Hotel Ambos Mundos (Both Worlds): Art
and Life? Hemingway, Room 511, just checked out
(of which, art or life?) My third Sazerac, memories
of Minsky's, while legs awaken salads in the brain,
and mine's a Waldorf now, Ouspensky's New Model
where time's a motion on some higher spatial plane,

(cinema, still photos moving in a dream of time)
and time's running out, compañero, a broken motion,
Icarus in flight. Love to Susan and bambino,

                                        Hart

Dear Lotte,
         Holed up in a hotel bar, I think
Cleveland Charlotte knows me well as anyone,
and when I wrote to you, "The true idea of God
is the only road to happiness," or something close
to that, please tell me what I meant. One morning,
drunk, Cathedral Santa Prisca, I climbed the tower,
rang the bell-rope that gathers God at dawn, though
no God, no waking pilgrims, just the local Law
and, I confess, a music, triple-tongued, vowels
inside of vowels, a kind of happiness. Love. Hart.

Dear Allen,
         "Le Bateau ivre" is prophetic, so now
why not The Bridge? Sometimes I fear it's just some sort
of spiritual boosterism for empire America.
And then there's Winters with his aesthetique morale:
form, meter as the reins to hold in check the wild horse
of the poem. But damn it, METER IS THE HORSE,
the very heartbeat of the horse, so drop the reins—
OK, I'm drunk, but word is more than word in that

or any poem, Jesus, I stood there, 3 a.m.,
on Roebling's cabled god, its welded, sculpted iron
embrace, staring at Manhattan, tears runneling
my face, the magnitude, the awful holiness
and pride of it, waves beating on the piers below,

Dear Grace,
            borne back ceaselessly into the past,
childhood poems you read to me each night and it
was language, diving down into the language, fall
through consonant and vowel, wash and wave of it,
etymology's dense, green growth, labyrinthine
mouths of history, one arc synoptic of all tides
below, O what lies deepest, meter of the sea,
surge and buffet of what's always underneath
and untranslatable, crucial, crux of everything,
unresurrected Christ, word, in the beginning
now endeth

Key to "Hart Crane in Havana"

I, too, dislike notes—much less a "key"—to poems, but in the case of a realistic imagining of Hart Crane's postcards, written the day before he leaped from the *Orizaba* to his death, such is unavoidable. In his letters it was natural for him, as for anyone writing to friends and relatives, to refer to shared knowledge, names, experiences that would be unknown to most outsiders. Therefore, for those who haven't read Paul Mariani's or Clive Fisher's very fine biographies of Crane, his correspondents as well as some of his allusions need to be identified. All the quoted lines in my poem are from Crane's poems, except for "borne back ceaselessly . . . ," which is taken from the famous final sentence of *The Great Gatsby*.

Wilbur: Wilbur Underwood, poet and government clerk in Washington, DC. He was an older, longtime friend and gay mentor to Crane.

Orizaba: The ship on which Crane and Peggy Cowley were returning to the USA.

Ramón Novarro, Hoover: Fisher reveals in his biography what while living in Pasadena, Crane received the sexual services of the film star, Ramón Novarro, as he had as an adolescent from the Hoover vacuum cleaner his mother, Grace, discovered him with.

Sambo: Sam Loveman, poet and publisher whom Crane met in his early twenties. Loveman was Crane's literary executor and published Brom Weber's *Hart Crane: A Biographical and Critical Study.*

iodine, Mercurochrome, Siqueiros: During his last days in Mexico, Crane made at least two suicide attempts and slashed his portrait by David Siqueiros with a razor blade.

Lawrence: D. H. Lawrence.

Hartley's tale, Albert Ryder: Crane's friend, the artist and poet, Marsden Hartley, tells this story of the painter, Albert Pinkham Ryder. Ryder's hostess asked him why he hadn't come to her Christmas dinner as he had promised, and he explained that he had indeed been there but had been standing outside the window, observing it.

Otto Kahn: Financier who generously underwrote Crane's expenses during the composition of *The Bridge*.

Bill: William Slater Brown. Novelist and translator, he and his wife were old friends of Crane, who had been a guest at their farmhouse in Dutchess County, New York, on several occasions.

Minsky's: The famous Manhattan burlesque theater that Crane and William Slater Brown frequented together and which was probably an influence on Crane's "National Winter Garden."

Ouspensky: Colleague of Gurdjieff and author of *Tertium Organum,* much read and discussed by Crane and his circle.

Lotte: Charlotte Rychtarik, a musician and painter, whom Crane had known since his early twenties in Cleveland.

Allen: Allen Tate, American literary critic and poet and a central member of the Fugitive group of southern poets. He was an early admirer of Crane's work.

"Le Bateau ivre": Rimbaud's famous poem is sometimes interpreted as prophesying the later events of his life.

Winters: Yvor Winters. Prominent literary critic who taught at Stanford University and like Allen Tate was an enthusiastic admirer and advocate of Crane's poetry.

Roebling: Both John Augustus Roebling, architect and builder of the Brooklyn Bridge, and his son, Washington Roebling, who continued his father's work and lived in the same apartment where Crane later wrote *The Bridge*.

Grace: Grace Hart Crane, the poet's mother, divorced from his father in 1917.

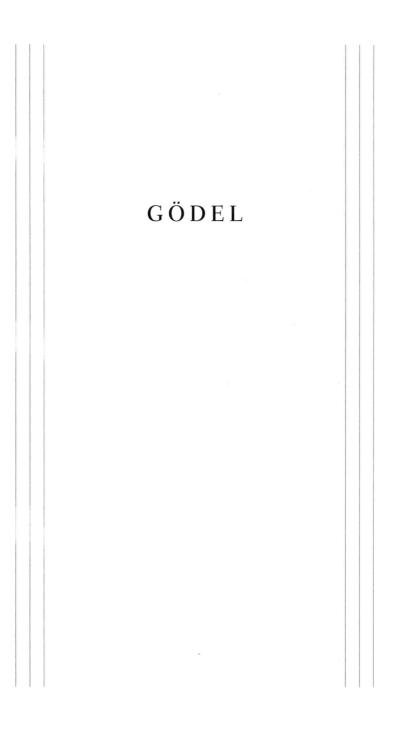

GÖDEL

The Cottonwood Lounge

It must follow that every infinity is, in a way
we cannot express, made finite to God.
                        —St. Augustine, *De Civitate Dei*

Four boys drinking tomato juice and beer
for God knows why, smoke from Pall Malls
guttering in the floor's red sawdust, the talk
the kind of mindless yak that foams up

when summer is wearing down, and Campbell
is already deep into Cantor and won't shut up,
lining up Coronas to the table's edge
to indicate "infinite progression, just imagine

they go on forever," but Travis, the sad one,
the maniac, who flunked out of A&M playing
bass in pickup bands and chasing girls, just
isn't having it, and says, "But the edge, Campbell,

is there and always will be," and Ira says,
"Please, asshole, just *imagine*," and so it goes,
integers, sets, *transfinite* sets, Coronas filling
the table because "with infinitely small Coronas

this table becomes, my friends, an infinite space
within finite limits," and Travis lip-synching
the Doors' "Break on Through" has carved
IRA CAMPBELL IS A DOUCHEBAG into the soft

lacquered tabletop, and time, illusion though it
may be, argues Ira, is walking past the table
in the form of Samantha Dobbins, all big hair
and legs and brown eyes like storms coming on

who I would date that summer and leave behind
and regret it even now, for time in its linear
progression, real or not, is, I fear, terribly finite,
as it is for God, who, looking down or up

or from some omnidirectional quantum point
in this one universe among many suffers
the idiocies of four beer-stunned boys stumbling
in the long confusion of their lives toward

what one might call the edge *that is there
and always will be,* for three have already found it,
and the one who has not ponders the mathematics
of the spirit, and Ira Campbell, who found God there.

Les Passages

The piano player at Nordstrom's was crying,
and no one knew what to do. His hands were thin
and pale as the starched cuffs that seemed to hold
his wrists above the keyboard until they collapsed
and lay there among the ache of his sobs and awful
silences and the tapping of cash registers, the ocean
of small voices, the hum and click of commerce.

We all stood there, looking at him, then away,
fine linen trousers hanging from our arms,
or scent of cologne we could not afford thickening
the air, or right foot half-slipped into the new blue shoe
we would not buy, not now, not ever, and those stiff
little cries kept coming, kept tumbling across
that immense, gleaming floor into the change rooms

where men and women were gazing into mirrors
far from this strange sadness that fell clumsily
into a day rushing like all days on earth to fulfill itself,
to complete like the good postman its mission, and so
we paused in the crumbling silence until the fragile,

cautious tones of "Autumn Leaves" began to drift
through the aisles and around the glittering display cases

as if a dream, a great dream, were being dreamed again,
and the cries of an infant rose now from the other end
of the mall, cries bursting into screams and then one long
scream that spread its wings and lifted, soaring,
and we grew thoughtful and began to move about again,
searching our pockets, wallets, purses, tooled leather
handbags for something that would stop that scream.

Wittgenstein, Dying

> *Someone who, dreaming, says, "I am dreaming," even if*
> *he speaks audibly in doing so, is no more right than if*
> *he said in his dream, "it is raining," while it was in fact*
> *raining. Even if his dream were actually connected*
> *with the noise of the rain.*
>
> —*On Certainty,* no. 676, written on his deathbed

The way a sentence is a story. *It is raining.*
Something happens, as the case may be, to something
of a certain kind and in a certain way.
Im Aufang war die Tat. In the beginning was
the act. So I tell a story: *it is raining.*
Grammar as a mirror of the world. Poor Trakl,
without a world except the world of words beyond
mere speech, drenched with dreams I never understood.
War, the nightmare of the earth, while in my backpack
Tolstoy's *Gospel* preached belief's old dream. I said,
once, *The sense of the world must lie outside the world.*
If that sense is "God," we might stand in His *rain,*
in "belief" of Him, but cannot quite get wet from it.
It is raining. In this room, the fire is blackening
the hearth's old stones, the now of my observing it
the only heaven of the mind. I said in my dream,
it is raining, but I dreamed the words themselves

and even that the words have meaning. Nonsense, then,
though now the rain is spattering the sixteen panes,
four by four, of my window. Keats, dying, looked out
a window at the Spanish Steps, Rome dimming in
the rain to gauzy nothing that must have seemed a dream,
like Madeline in his poem on St. Agnes' Eve.
Porphyro lying next to her spoke himself *into*
her dream, the voice she heard as *known* as the hand
of Moore showing the other one exists: "Here is one hand."
Because all certainty at least *begins* with the body's
certainty. My brother, Paul, playing Brahms,
feels his amputated arm, his hand, still moving.
Can the body *know*? Can, therefore, the mind?
Thought is the mind minding, poetry the mind
embodied, what cannot be spoken, that is, *explained*:
these curtains—Burano lace, I think—that sift
the April light, walls papered with lurid rose designs,
a bird in the window's lower panes resting on
a branch. In Ireland, chaffinches feeding
from my hand. With what certainty! "Here is one
hand." *It is raining.* And if I say, *I am dying,*
within this finite life enclosed at either end
by the unknowable, what are my words—
not a knowing, surely, but a kind of wonder
bodied forth here where the Cambridge rain comes down
on Storeys Way in a house called Storeys End.

The Barber

*The barber shaves all and only men who do not
shave themselves. Who shaves the barber?*

—Bertrand Russell's paradox

I have been waiting so long . . . little pocks
of rust freckle the shanks of my best blades.
Who, after all, would be shaved by a barber
boasting foliage of such grotesque proportions,
dragging its damp, heavy life along sidewalks
and alleyways, doomed to this eternal algebra
of existence, these parallel universes
of paradox where bearded and beardless
coexist simultaneously and separately
and my twin in his timeless moment stands
mirrored in the lather of despair, blade
scraping flesh forever barren. Between us:
nothing, a space infinite and infinitessimal,
the sunless, silent arctic zone of contradiction.
On my side Cretans always lie; on his,
the lies are always true. On my side, particles;
on his, waves. A life unimaginable, but a life.

My wife—anguished, disgusted—long since done
with making love to Sherwood Forest, amused

herself with knitting it into increasingly
bizarre shapes, single rope ladders at first,
then interconnected hair suits for a trio
of monkeys. She lives in Alexandria now
with a Greek financier, a balding man of pink,
pampered countenance who offered me thousands
to shave. He sympathized. He saw in me the fate
of the common world lugging its debts and losses
through the streets like a black beard of shame,
the clean face of prosperity ever disappearing
until the man disappears, a walking shadow,
a beard bearing a man, a man engulfed
in the chaos of his own flesh, his own hair.

The razor strops of fate hang uselessly
beside their cruel mirrors. Among the dazzle
of chrome embellishments, bottles of Wildroot
and cans of Rose Pomade cry *Traitor!*
to my lank tresses, and old customers,
victims themselves of cut-rate solitudes
in downtown hotels, wander by with lowered eyes
and trembling hands. Shaggy children gawk
and scatter when they spy in the shop's
deep shadows a chair of hair, a breathing mound
multiplied infinitely in mirrors facing mirrors.

My only solace is a dream, a tonsorial fantasy
that more and more possesses me, of a world
in which the calculus of being demands that

barbers shave only men who shave themselves.
In it my twin and I stand handsomely behind
our chairs, he sporting a small goatee,
my nude visage chaste as an egg, immaculately
conceived, saintly in its pure nakedness,
and an entire cosmos of the newly shaven,
redolent with lotions but somehow needing
our final caresses and fleshly blessings,
lines the boulevard. The sun is shining.
The brick streets glow richly. And beside me
my wife prepares the secret oils of annointment
and reaches up to stroke my silken chin.

Hume

for Peter Caws

> *. . . experience only teaches us, how one event constantly*
> *follows another; without instructing us in the secret connexion,*
> *which binds them together, and renders them inseparable.*
>
> —David Hume,
> *An Enquiry Concerning Human Understanding*

Philosophia: declining Kansas light
lifting dust motes from the shadows, scars
along the prewar plaster walls of Frazier Hall.
Professor Caws, left hand raised against the sun,
right hand mapping on the board each turn
and pivot in Hume's argument against
causality. Hume's game, like mine,
is pool: one ball strikes another, and between
the two, says Caws, *nada*, nothing but
coincidence. And forget the thousand times
it happens, that little sad inductive leap.
I'm stunned. A, then B. And between them, what,
some vast, flat plain of pure event where things
just happen—a bird falling from the sky,
a distant shout, a cow wandering along
the highway's shoulder, the sun here, then there,

the moon full or empty, a white boat floating
on a sea of wheat.
                    That's it: a sea between
two countries: the land of *Cause*, like Iceland,
clean, uncluttered, a kind of purple mist
hanging in the air, a few cold souls caught
in mid-stride on a frozen lake, the awful silence,
trees that fall without a sound, and across the bay,
Effect, marching bands in every street,
unruly crowds, that balmy island climate,
and the thick, melodic accents of its citizens
that make you think of Istanbul, or wine,
or tile floors in geometrical designs—
and in between, the sea, soundless but for
the crash of waves, since nothing happens there
except the constant passage, back and forth,
of the little boat called the Logic of Induction
that never reaches shore. And there it is
in the distance—listing, it seems to me—
its pilot, nameless and alone, slumped
across the wheel.
                    Walking out of class,
breathing in the cold, salt air of Hume,
I turn to Anderson, our point guard:
"You no-talent hack, you're just a servant
of coincidence. Take that to the NBA."
"I'll drink to that," he says, and so we head
for Duck's, a game of pool, and look across

that flat green field, listening to the click
and thump of billiard balls, studying
the angles, as our ignorant young lives
pass slowly like the evening sun, unmoved,
unmoving, that sinks below the Kansas plain.

Gödel

So here is Campbell, murky, shadow-blotched
beneath the backroom table lamp at Duck's,
first one of us to dig past proposition 4.2
in the *Tractactus,* Dante's true disciple,
unfurling long verbal tapestries by heart
from *Purgatorio* (the dullest parts,
perversely), Haig & Haig in hand, always,
it seemed to me, in darkened rooms—scarred,
name-carved booths in downtown college bars,
jazz joints in Kansas City where after Reed
and the Sorbonne he played lounge piano
at the Muhlebach, claimed to know the mob
("'double-entry bookkeeping,' Lansky said,
'was Western culture's breakthrough'"), argued
Plotinus held the key to quantum mystery,
Gödel's madness proved the end of thought.

The end of thought! And then the cosmic sweep
of hands, smile's exploding nova, eyes two moons
across that smoke-burdened, blue neon room—
a kind of storm, or far, Cartesian weather.
Shapeless forms balloon inside a lava lamp
above the Wurlitzer's warped, ancient Coltrane,
"Body and Soul"—"the music of *becoming,*"

Campbell says, "Plato's spiral of ascent
toward the Forms, the unattainable,
the way those chords unravel, then take flight . . ."
His voice wobbles, trails off, vanishes
beneath the gathering cloud of his cigar,
then floats back up, "Gödel, you see, had proved
no system is complete or closed, no life
contains its own clear validation." Arms
waving, he heads back into the kitchen
where he washes dishes now and lives
behind the Texaco across the street, among
his books, and thinks about the end of thought.

FIVE
PROSE POEMS
FROM THE
JOURNALS OF
ROY ELDRIDGE
GARCIA

Piano

The blind piano tuner had come to the wrong address. I said, "I'm very sorry. You must have the wrong address." He insisted on seeing the piano, though I have none. I showed him the living room, which was being recarpeted. "A Bösendorfer! Wonderful! One of the finest! What an opportunity!" He was overjoyed, talking at length about its virtues, second to none—the crisp, clean tone, silken touch, huge bass, marvelous sustain, and so forth. He took out his tuning kit and began immediately. He claimed to have heard Schnabel play the entire Beethoven sonata cycle on one in Royal Albert Hall in London. After a short time, he played a chord. "Hear that? Wonderful. So rich." I told him I could hear nothing, and he nodded sympathetically, even sadly, saying that to lose one's sense of hearing was to lose a portion of one's soul. "In his last days, Beethoven heard with his fingertips, I truly believe that," he muttered to himself. To hear him soliloquize rhapsodically about the piano and the great performers he had heard—"Hoffman with his small hands would have loved this light action, like angel wings," or "Perfect for Lipatti and his Chopin, so fluid and transparent"—was almost to hear the music itself, to be seated in the concert hall, center of the third row, to feel the tremble of the young woman's shoulder in the adjacent seat, her barely repressed sighs in the crescendos of the "Appassionata," that unearthly, mystical moment between the dying of the last note and the avalanche of applause. His devotion to the Bösendorfer, the obsessive attention to every detail of the tuning process, preoccupied him for most of the afternoon, and I served him coffee, then afterward offered him a martini in celebration of a job well done. "You're a lucky man, such a fine instrument," he said, as if to the piano itself, as he left. Yes, I am, I thought, and looked back at the living room the way Beethoven must have looked at that young woman in the third row, her tear-filled eyes, the slightly parted lips, her hands pressed together as if in prayer.

Los Angeles, 1957

Cendrars

Blaise, Maria, and I were walking toward the Seine from his
apartment on the rue Montaigne, and he was speaking of
Apollinaire, Captain Lacroix, Abel Gance, and others, his
planned biography of Mary Magdalene, his beloved son, Remy,
whose plane was shot down in WWII, Blaise's experience
in WWI, the loss of his right arm. And he mentioned the
phantom limb sensation, the pain of it, as if the arm were still
there, that it is like memory, the memory that will not quite go
away, that it is in effect the body's memory, but more, that it is
like poetry, the phantom life: not there in any material way, yet
intensely there to the reader, the amputee who has lost some
nameless yet essential limb of existence, probably on the long,
dark path out of childhood. Teary-eyed with excitement, the
reader can say of the poem, *yes,* this is *life,* or better, this is the
life *within* life, but try to convince the passerby, the onlooker,
who will simply observe the empty sleeve flapping in the wind
and shake his head sadly. Then he returned to his favorite
subject, the levitation of saints, much as he had spoken of it in
Le Lotissement du ciel years before, and Paris rose around us as
if for the first time—the sun like the oranges of the surrealists
plunging into the Seine, the wild applause of the chestnut
trees, the truncated towers of Notre Dame—and Maria looked

at me and smiled that odd, worried smile that is still with me. Whose pain will not leave. A plane falling out of the sky. That phantom smile.

Aix-en-Provence, 1952

The Deer

Amid the note cards and long, yellow legal pads, the late
nineteenth-century journals containing poems by Swinburne or
Rossetti or Lionel Johnson, the Yeats edition of Blake with its
faded green cover and beveled edges, I and the other readers in
the British Library began to feel an odd presence. We lifted our
eyes in unison to observe the two small deer that had entered
the room so quietly, so very discreetly, the music of their
entering suspended above us, inaudible, but there, truly, as the
deer were there. They paused, we could hear their breathing,
or so it seemed, and no one moved. What could we do, there
were deer in the room, and now hundreds of deer reflected in
our eyes. The silence was unbearable at first, and the librarian
in the linen blouse, her long fingers trembling, began to weep.
The deer sensed this and, without seeming to move at all,
came closer, licking her elbows, sniffing the soapy fragrance
in the well of her neck, staring into her watery eyes. At some
point beyond memory we could no longer distinguish her from
the deer, it was all stillness anyway, everywhere the silence
covered us like a silken net, and the books began to darken and
crumble with age. We had all found our place, our eyes were
full of deer, and our sadness was without cease.

Paris, 1953

Working Men in Their Sunday Clothes

They lean against their unwashed pickups. The streets are
empty, houses silent, scrub oaks bent over porches like old
women over stoves or hunters gathered around a fallen deer.
One of the men chews Red Man and stares down at the sky
mirrored in his Marine Corps dress shoes from Parris Island
twenty years ago. His three boys with their scrubbed faces
stare up at him, and he thinks of himself as a boy, his mother
running the comb through his hair while he listened for the
Santa Fe on its morning run, or his grandmother's lace curtains
in late afternoon, that grid of light. The second wears a bolo tie,
its turquois slide polished and set in silver by his grandfather,
Justin boots dull with red dust, washed and creased jeans, and
a National Feed cap which he places over his coffee thermos
in the front seat. The church is familiar as his own house or his
garage, saw blades mounted on the wall like giant coins, tools
in their painted profiles above the worktable. The gold crucifix
beneath his shirt was given at confirmation, and he always
touches it three times after reading to his daughter at night.
Leno, the third, twists the buttons of his best jean jacket,
kept clean for Sundays. When Yolanda waves to him from the
church porch, her hair flares in the wind the way it does in the
truck on the way home along the white caliche road, through
open fields, and he remembers the old farm, the well he dug
with his uncles, the first water flowing muddy, then cold, clear,

almost blue. One evening driving Johnson Road he looked at the oil refinery in heavy snow, columns of pale smoke lifting into the night sky porous and quick with stars, and thought it beautiful. Out hunting one day, the three of them saw a hawk lurch suddenly in mid-flight and fall helplessly to earth. They think of their lives as long highways tapering away, then disappearing into the sandhills. It is Sunday. God for them is a carpenter with bruised fingernails.

Liberal, Kansas, 1961

The Creature from the Black Lagoon

Midnight movie. Entering the theater, the usher's flashlight
clearing the way. The *going down into,* the descent. Dante. The
ten steps down into the Conciergerie, antechamber of death,
the guillotine nightmares that must have filled that enormous,
cavernous room. The New York subway, where Billy Batson
in some gloomy, hidden side-passage received the powers
of SHAZAM. And last night that old B movie, silly as it was
predictable, except for one unforgettable shot underwater:
the creature, the fish-man, swimming beneath and parallel
to the beautiful woman from the boat as she twists, sleek,
undulant, feet fluttering, gliding in that white swimsuit across
the lagoon's surface, then shattering it, light bursting all around
her. And he follows, almost mimicking her movements. The
camera sees her as he does: a glow, a charisma, the supple arch
of her body, its curves and hollows, as she dips and rises. And
there is the usher, a boy, staring hard at the screen, hypnotized
by her beauty, the water's spangle, the dark monstrous thing
lurking just below her. We all watch with the eyes of that boy
the shining life of this film—the way we sometimes look at
works of art, the way I stood years ago before that Cézanne still
life at the Orangerie. We wake astonished in a suddenly fixed
moment of our lives. We are swimming toward something—

something bright, something of promise, something *not
ourselves*—reaching out, then pulling back, here, in the dark
below, in our underworld.

Liberal, Kansas, 1960

THE
BEAUTY
OF
ABANDONED
TOWNS

In memory of O.T. and Nellie Swearingen

. . . labor omnia vicit
improbus et duris urgens in rebus egestas.

—Virgil, *Georgics*

The Beauty of Abandoned Towns, *prose*

> *Finally we sold out—you know, the big farm eats*
> *the small farm.*
>
> —Edna Pforr, Hamberg, North Dakota

> *. . . ruins do not speak; we speak for them.*
>
> —Christoper Woodward, *In Ruins*

Jefferson, Marx, and Jesus. Looking back, you can hardly believe it.

Bindweed and crabgrass shouldering through asphalt cracks,
rats scuttling down drainpipes, undergrowth seething with
grasshoppers.

The bumper crop in 1929. I stood on the front porch, dawn
rolling over me like a river baptism because I was a new man in
a new world, a stand of gold and green stretching from my hands
to the sun coming up. In a way, a mirage. We bought a house in
town. There it is. Or was.

The water tower, taller than the copper domes of Sacred Heart
in Leoville, silhouette flooding the football field, missing boards
of the scavenged bleachers, minor prophecies: *Bobby + Pam*
forever, Panthers rule, peace now.

Presence is absence, says the philosopher. The future devours the
past. Look at the goatgrass and ragweed claiming the feed store.

Sunflowers banging their heads on a conclusion of brick, the
wind's last argument lost in a yellow cloud.

Eugene Debs set up The People's College in Fort Scott. Meridel
Le Sueur grew up there. It lasted three years. Imagine: Comrade
Debs, Comrade Sheppard, Comrade Le Sueur. In Kansas.

The open windows of the high school no longer surprise,
pigeons flying in and out, the dumb cry of blackboards, wooden
desks hauled away with the carved names of the long absent,
the lost, the dead, the escaped.

The Farmer's Alliance tried. Socialist farm policy was for them
a straight road to Jefferson's democracy. But they were always
blocked by the big landowners. The deal breaker was profits, not
politics. The harvest was topsoil, not wheat.

The last hitching post. The last horse, I suppose. Like Sunday
morning, the last hymn, the last person to hear the last hymn.
May the circle be unbroken. The circle is broken.

We subscribed to the Haldeman-Julius Appeal to Reason,
published out of little Girard, Kansas. Our children grew up on
his Little Blue Books. The Federalist Papers, Thoreau, Emerson,
Marx, Ingersoll, Upton Sinclair.

The clapboard stores, slats long ago sand-blasted in dust
storms, bleached or ochre now, gray, the faint green and yellow
of a Lipton Tea ad on red brick. Broken windows flashing the
setting sun in a little apocalypse of light, blind men in shades
staring at the horizon, waiting for a sign. Stillness everywhere.

You know, you're wasting your time. No one gives a shit about
this. None of it. No one.

Dearth of cars, motion, grind of gears, noise of commerce,
chatter and cry of farm kids dangling from the beds of
rusted-out pickups, murmur and guffaw of old men outside
the Savings and Loan, stories, jokes. Quiet as a first snow.
Somewhere a dog barks. A wire gate slams shut.

I'm so goddamned old I still tense up when an afternoon sky
darkens. A roller would come in, dust up to eight thousand feet. If
you were in the field, you were lost until it cleared. Or dead from
suffocation. Where was your family? Where were your children?

Houses with tin roofs, wrap-around porches for watching
thunderstorms, most vacant but here and there pickup
windows flaming in sunset, trimmed lawn, history in forty years
of license plates nailed to the garage wall. Cellar door. Swing
set, that little violin screech of rusted chains, hush of evening,
choir of cicadas. The living among the dead.

It started when agriculture professors began to teach farming as a business rather than a vocation. And then the big ones over the years ate the little ones. But in this country vocations are exploited. Ask the public school teachers.

The lords of grain: two cats fat on field mice lounge beneath the elevator steps where dust from a caliche road powders them white—wraiths, or white surrender flags.

On the other hand, subsidies can kill small farms these days. Back then we were desperate. Our children were hungry. FDR kept us alive. Then something went wrong. Big got bigger, small died. Still dying, hanging on but bedridden. The Ogallala aquifer's almost tapped out. I mean, for God's sake.

Between the boarded bank and the welding shop husks drift like molted feathers or the sloughed scales of cottonmouths. Weeds waist-high shade the odd shoe still laced, a Coke carton bleeding into bluestem, dulled scraps of newsprint that say who died in Ashland or Sublette or Medicine Lodge.

It goes back to the oikos, *the Greek family farm. Some ethic, some code of honor, kept them small. Big was vulgar, immoral. The Romans, too. Cato the Elder, rich as Joe Kennedy, taught his son agronomy, not commerce.*

They are not haunted. They are not the "ghosts of themselves." They are cousin to vanishing, to disappearance. They are the highway that runs through them.

The picture show shut down decades ago. That's where we saw the world, the world our children and grandchildren ran off to. What happens when a nation loses its agrarian populace? My grandson worked as an usher there. He's a poet now. We have more poets than farmers. I don't think that's what Jefferson had in mind.

Not even decline, but the dawn of absence. Architecture of the dead. The lives they housed are dust, the wind never stops.

A disproportionate percentage of the American soldiers killed in Iraq are from small rural towns. The farmer/soldier, foundation of the Greek polis. Fodder for war. Blood harvest.

The wind never stops. *Our children were hungry.* The highway's long blade under the sun. *Something went wrong.* The towns are empty. *The circle is broken.*

Household

. . . *the poetry of the house.*

—Gaston Bachelard

Tornado-flattened, water pump still standing,
iron handle bent straight back, then later,
a duck's bill found buried in the Dutch elm
overhanging what had been the chicken coop.
But now, again, a house: five rooms, kitchen window
that held the morning sun in summer, jar
of cold cream on the sill, a coffee cup, chipped,
bearing CARLSBAD CAVERNS and a scene of stalactites
looming sometimes in broken dreams. Summers,
naked to the waist, she sipped cold coffee
washing dishes, lifting now and then the dishcloth
to her breasts, wearing August's heavy heat
like a winter coat. Across the side yard leaned
the separator shed and in between, perhaps,
that rare, odd moment: mousers stalking
scraps of paper fluttering in tall grass,
a meadowlark bearing catkins in its beak
to pad a barn nest. Farther on, the barn's
small night, and she could stare straight through
its open doors to the horse corral, imagining

the creek below spangled black and silver
under sunlight, flashing laughter from someone's
children leaping into memory.
                              The big room:
her mother's bureau, two pine rockers, upright piano
pushed against the south wall with a Chopin étude
she could never master. After reading
Willa Cather's book that fall, she cried for days.
To leave Nebraska. To live in music. *My God.*
Playing for the choir in church, she watched
her too large hands. The preacher's voice bore
a hollowness, some dry and empty space
between his words that made her want to slap him.

She had never seen the sea, imagining instead
the red maize blue, its scrolling waves, volute,
hungry. A dust storm brought dirt thick enough
to shovel from the screened-in sleeping porch so
she swept then lay down on the floor and lolled
her head side to side watching little dust clouds rise,
fall, rise like the red dust plumage of her husband's
tractor, notes of the piano drifting through
the side yard as she strolled through the cavern
every morning that cool darkness stalactites
damp against her fingertips *home is where
the heart is* what nonsense *home is four walls
five rooms* space for a mind and her mind was
a house   attic   bedroom   kitchen   big room

cellar *the mind was a house* and gazing next day
out the window a new sun stroking her neck
that way the sun as it had been explained
to her the seething boiling gases rushing up
tornadoes everywhere but no fire no fire at all

Bloom School

In 1936 dust storms would clot
the mortar of its bricks, but now the wind
sweeps clean its crumbling, fluted columns
and pollinates a field of bluestem
and sunflowers tall as high school kids.
Nothing is everywhere: doorless doorways,
dirt-filled foundations, and weed-pocked
sidewalks leading to a sky that blued
the eyes of bored students stupefied
by geometry and Caesar's Latin.

Gallia est omnis divisa in partes tres.
Who cared how Gaul's dead past was divvied up?
Every radio in every car in Bloom
cried *Now,* and now was an eternity
except at graduation when the future
was invented by the Baptist minister.
The stars that evening fell on main street
and sank into our laminated hoods
streaked with downtown lights, and heaven
once more rolled across our rolling lives.

My wife and I made love here last night.
I manage kitchenware at Wal-Mart,

and sometimes the future rides my back the way
I rode my rented combine years ago.
So Ann and I will come here evenings when
a fat moon floats in absent hallways, their lost,
remembered voices rising through the stillness,
and in other rooms students struggle over
Euclid's arcs and circles and bend to translate
the vanished past into another tongue.

The Teller

The bank so buried under hungry shrubs,
snakeweed, and creeper reaching even
to the carved stone BANK ESTABLISHED 1910
that its octagonal rust brick seems to shirk
a street long gone.
                 Where is he now,
Mr. Spivey, the only teller, who lived
above STATE FARM and had a wife in Blue Creek
he never saw? What led him there?
What kept her in a darkness we could
only wonder at? Men lived with wives,
we thought, the new moon rose, snow fell,
and familiar as a thumb each Sunday
Mr. Spivey sang the solo parts in choir,
angelically, our mothers said.
                      Fridays,
staying late, he cashed our paychecks,
small hands counting out and pushing
stacks of new bills crisp as corn sheaves
beneath the cage. Smiling through the bars,
he called us *mister,* as I, oddly, call him now.
Good evening, Mr. Elwood. Good day, Mr. Smith,
the words thin and lyrical as the paper
whispering in our ears.

                    Coming from the PALACE
those nights, we would sometimes see his shadow
in the risen window on the square, the streets
of Edward Hopper dimly lit below where
people walked and laughed and talked
about new money earned and saved or spent.
All across America there must have been
such streets and such men who touched
the people's hands with money and lived alone.

Leaving

> *Leaving the ark-tight farm in its blue and mortgaged*
> *weather . . .*
>
> —Thomas McGrath,
> *Letter to an Imaginary Friend*

The scrub oaks beyond my window
slipped, tree by tree, into fog,
ice lacquering the black branches
that dipped and clattered in the wind
making random flashes, the flicker
of street lamps in Paris, perhaps,
or the Gauloises of crowds at the Dome
with their red wine and blue copies
of *Ulysses*, fires along the Seine.

The fog sprawled across the fields
of my father's farm that rolled
and blundered through low-lying hills
and gulleys to a dusty creek, damp
only when winter wheat was bogged
in snow. From my bed, moored among
bubbling vials of medicinal ethers,
I would wander the creek, winding
through bluestem and dogwood,

wander its length outward, standing
at last high above the great cities
of Europe and their thousand lights
dreamed in the long sleep, distant
and deep, of dusk in winter. Now
was the leaving, the motion outward,
to rise, to pull myself at last from
the thickening air of sickness, to walk
into fog and the world inside the fog.

Wheat

For in the night in which he was betrayed,
he took bread.

In Clyde, Missouri, the Benedictine Sisters
of Perpetual Adoration cut unleavened bread
into communion wafers and gather them

in plastic bags folded, stapled, and later packed
in boxes. After Compline the sisters rise again
from prayers, lie down upon their narrow beds,

and wait for sleep's wide wings to fold around them.
Their hands still give the light sweet smell of bread,
and loaves like little clouds drift through their dreams,

wafers raining down to make a blizzard
of the Word made flesh, *Corpus Christi,*
of God's own Son. On evening break at Wal-Mart

Doris Miller spreads ketchup on her Big Mac
and salts her fries, time and wages swallowed
like a sacrament, eternity the dregs

that throng and cluster in the shallows
of her complimentary Styrofoam cup.
At the Exxon next door, Walter Miller

lifts his pickup's hood, then turns to stare
at the acreage he used to own across the road.
Was *his* wheat, he wonders, even the smallest grain

in its long ascent to final form, ever changed into
the body of our Lord? The Benedictine Sisters
of Perpetual Adoration wake to Matins, prayers

that rise like crane migrations over feedlots,
packing houses, hog farms, the abandoned small
stores of Leeton, the Dixon Community Center,

the Good Samaritan Thrift Shop in Tarkio.
A gravel road veers toward the Open Door Cafe,
windows boarded up and painted powder blue

and lemon Day-Glow, perpetual sunrise on
a town silent as the absent cry of starlings
or idle irrigation pumps rusting in the dust

of August, where the plundered, corporate earth
yields the bread placed in the outstretched palms,
take and eat, of the citizens of Clyde, Missouri.

The Church of the New Jerusalem, Pawnee Rock, Kansas

North across the tracks and past the fallen GANO
in a gaggle of shacks and collapsing farm homes
huddled in their groves of windbreaks, the church
of Immanuel Swedenborg shoulders live oak branches
ancient as the tribes of Kansas or the sorrow notes
of thrumming fence wire. It blesses with the spirit
of William Blake's unlettered wife the wrecked,
abandoned husks of tractors, doorless pickups,
and the odd, half-buried hearse in someone's long
backyard gone to cheatgrass and rusted oil cans
across the road.

                Catherine Blake walks the crumbling
WPA sidewalks through the diminished town,
and her husband's dark and fallen seraphim
are mares' tails in the pearl-gray skies of dusk.
She was the midwife of Blake's illuminations,
and when one year later they escaped the Church
of the New Jerusalem, he prophesied that heaven
and hell would marry, his demons and Swedenborg's
too lucid cherubs embracing in an ecstasy of love
and irony.

          Without contraries is no progression,
the disappearing town of Pawnee Rock rigid

in its long descent into the unforgiving past.
MAGNETO-ELECTRIC leans against the closed P.O.
and on the west GARY'S AUTO SERVICE lets the wind
keen and rasp through half-boarded windows.
In Catherine's thrift shop at closing time
the angels of memory inhabit every garment
to enter once again the streets of commerce,
rich Saturdays of trade and barter, Mennonites
in black wagons where towheads gawked
and mouthed in rural wonder the songs
of innocence, the old men on the corner spitting
Red Man and unraveling tales of better days and
shrewder men, land cleared and furrowed, boasting
rain follows the plow, the dream that came undone.

We share the bumper of my car to sit and watch
the congregation of eleven leaving Swedenborg's
basilica, voices lifted now in loud good-byes
as the bus rumbles onto Main Street and beyond.

And this is visionary Kansas: the last believers
plunged back into a night where the angels
of a Lutheran engineer rise above Wal-Mart
and the corporate fields of chemicals and wheat.
And two hard skeptics speak into the hollow streets
of vanishing, the emptiness that follows ruin,
the vagrant ways of memory and mental flight,
and the garments that clothed the backs

of women who, like her, signed their names
carefully with an X and saw the New Jerusalem
in a vision real as the land could give
and then slowly take away, false as prophecy.

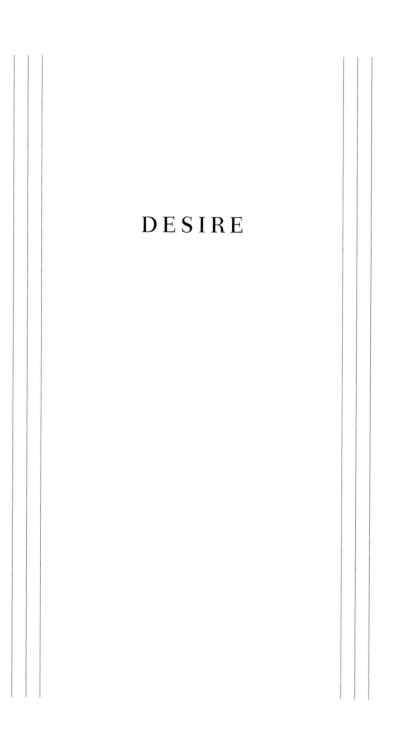

DESIRE

Madonna and Child, Perryton, Texas, 1967

A litter of pickups nose into Sancho's Market
south of town late Friday night rinsed in waves
of pink neon and samba music from some station
in Del Rio spilling out across the highway.
Sancho's wife dances alone behind the cash box
while her daughter, Rosa, tries to quiet her baby
whose squalls rip through the store like a weed cutter
shredding the souls of the carnal, the appetitious,
indeed the truly depraved as we in our grievous
late-night stupor and post-marijuana hunger
curse the cookie selection and all its brethren
and Al yells at Leno lost among the chips,
beef jerky, string cheese, *bananas* for Chrissakes,
that if he doesn't stop now and forever telling
Okie jokes he will shoot his dog who can't hunt
anyway so what the hell, but the kid is unreal,
a cry ascending to a shriek, then a kind
of rasping roar, the harangue of the gods,
sirens cleaving the air, gangs of crazed locusts
or gigantic wasps that whine and ding our ears
until the air begins to throb around us
and a six-pack of longnecks rattles like snakes
in my hand. And then poor Rosa is kissing
its forehead, baby riding her knee like a little boat

lost at sea, and old Sancho can't take it either,
hands over his ears, *Dios mio, ya basta! Dios mio,*
so Rosa opens her blouse, though we don't look,
and then we do, the baby sucking away, plump cheeks
pumping, billowing sails of the *Santa Maria*
in a high wind, the great suck of the infinite
making that little *nick, nick* sound, Rosa
smiling down, then Sancho turns off the radio
and we all just stand there in the light and shadow
of a flickering fluorescent bulb, holding
our sad little plastic baskets full of crap,
speechless and dying a little inside as Rosa
whispers *no llores, no llores, mija, mijita,*
no llores, and the child falls asleep, lips
on breast, drops of milk trickling down,
we can even hear it breathing, hear ourselves
breathing, the hush all around and that hammer
in our chests so that forty years later
this scene still hangs in my mind, a later work,
unfinished, from the workshop of Zurbarán.

Desire

I want! I want!

—William Blake

Desire is endless.
Singing to the moon,
you think it will sink
softly into your arms.
After a hot spasm of love,
you think, that was good,
but it could have been better.
On Saturday nights in Snyder
all the drunks came to the big red
revival tent to be cured.
Later they would celebrate,
singing "Your Cheatin' Heart"
and passing around a bottle of Southern Comfort.
Earl Penney in Las Vegas
won big, lost it all,
and in ecstasy and song
slammed his car into a concrete wall.
So, people keep taking out garbage
every Monday and Thursday.

It never stops. There they go
in their pajamas, cursing
the cold pavement under their feet.

What He Said

When Candi Baumeister announced to us all
that J.D. was *in love* with Brigitte Bardot,
drawing those two syllables out like some kid
stretching pink strands of Dubble Bubble
from between her teeth, J.D. chose not
to duck his head in the unjust shame
of the truly innocent but rather lifted it
in the way of his father scanning the sky
in silent prayer for the grace of rain abundant
upon his doomed soybeans or St. Francis
blessing sparrows or the air itself, eyes radiant
with Truth and Jesus, and said, *Babydoll,*
I would walk on my tongue from here to Amarillo
just to wash her dishes.
                         There is a time
in the long affliction of our spoken lives when,
among all the verbal bungling, stupidity,
and general disorder that burden us
like the ragged garment of the flesh itself, when,
beneath the vast and articulate shadows
of the saints of language, the white dove of genius
with its quick, wild wings has entered our souls,
our immaculate ignorance, and we are,
at last, redeemed. And so is conceived and born

the thing said, finally, *well*—nay, *perfectly*—
as it might be said by that unknowable Being
for whom we have in our mortal linguistic
incapacity no adequate name except the one
Candi Baumeister bore in her own virginal
moment of absolute poetry: *My God, J.D.*

Poetry Night at the Frost Place

for Donald Sheehan

The bear speaks:

These humans never tire of speaking love.
I have seen them gathered here at night
in their great loneliness and I in mine
near the forest's edge. The light falling

from the barn lifts them from the lawn,
then someone speaks, and all are drawn inside
to listen. And something in the words,
some old deep thing like fire, leaves these creatures

motionless and hushed as deer in winter,
waiting tense and watchful in that ancient pool
of light until the beasts, too, begin, one by one,
to stand and listen in the dark as I do now.

Night Terrors

DOOR OPENED FOR NEW ERA OF
NUCLEAR ARMS
—*Los Angeles Times*, May 10, 2003

And here they come again, 4 a.m.,
gaggle of shadows, thick wallow
of groans, sodden bleak wailings

blown like an explosion of grackles
from my small life's basement, Bosch-like
in their fury, their perverse pink rage,

and ending always in that great white flash.
My cup of decaf rattles in its saucer
like the hooves of distant horses from

those Saturday afternoon Westerns
I saw as a boy, afterward walking
straight into the flame of day, blinded,

hands over my eyes, stunned, stumbling
away from that world of perfect justice
and brave men and virtuous women

and the violence that ends violence
as it does not ever in this world
and so what's the difference, night
or day, that's my problem, Dr. Stein.

Moth

A moth devoured words.

—The Exeter Book

A larval tunneling between pages.
  Gorged on print,
wallowing in pulp, it falls into the long

sleep that later breaks and frays as wings
  sluggish as oars
begin to bludgeon the heavy air,

baffled by walls of dusk and lugging
  the soft body
toward a squall of light. Dun wings

flail, ribbed like Gothic vaults and
  camouflaged with moons
large as owl eyes. Lurching through

the light's rain, it veers, collides,
  hugs the bulb
and falls away. And the singed antennae

recall in something like a mezzotint
  the larval dark passage,
the hunger, the gray dream of *with, and, the.*

Final Exam

The gluey armpits, underwear in knots, coffee grounds
riding snowmobiles through the brain circuits, and insane
mental spasms heaving Samantha Dobbins, my first love,
onto p. 126 of *The Divine Comedy* which I have now not read
four times while I reach for the bra snap and her tongue
slithers into my ear shouting NO SCHOOL TOMORROW!
FREE MONEY! although embracing the angels of Purgatory,
Dante grabs a truckload of empty air and who can remember
all those names anyway, Count Mozzarella, Guido,
Duke of Ferrara, Linguini of Padua, Carol Calabrese
who used to glide her fingertips across the back of my neck
in Mr. Ely's geometry class with the static cutting like
a bandsaw through my favorite station, desk lamp blazing
into my forehead, can of beer beneath it turning to horse piss
in its ascent up the plateau of boredom where Virgil directs
Dante's pious attention to THE UNPREPARED chewing on
horse blankets for who knows, forever, or until they can
maneuver their dad's Buick Dynaflow behind Bailey's barn
off Highway 80 and oh God she has draped something silky
over the rearview mirror and is giggling into the next county
where the coffeepot is way empty, only the brown rings
of absence and crumbs of Fritos lugged on the backs of

THE PROCRASTINATORS as they crawl backward into the muddy lake of TOMORROW, but listen to KPRG, what a great station, it's Ethel Merman, *I'll build a stairway to paradise* . . .

Les Saltimbanques au repos

Cigarettes, white coffee cups,
laughter like dimes poured from a glass jar.

At Modell's each Sunday morning
the ancient ones gather
to make their old wives laugh,
or no one at all, here, or on park benches,
watching the parade of strollers,
or the sleepers, or leaves that skitter like applause.

It was a kind of sleep, the old days,
the fall into the vague familiar,
a story unfolding slowly, the laughter,
then the waking to a copper scattering
of sunlight across the walls, mirror,
the blue jacket from the night before,
the lucky one, draped across the chair.

And so they are kind to one another, generous,
that bit about the drunk in the morgue, wonderful,
old men in their craft
or the memory of it, prey to jealousy
and failure and the seductions of success,
the applause that never dies, that dream.

They leave large tips,
trying to outdo each other, yet helping
with coats, canes, a wheelchair
for the eldest, to whom they all defer.

It is almost noon,
the room given back to murmur,
music of glass and silverware.
Outside, the city's life is thin, ragged,
a riddle needing sometimes to be unraveled,
the opposite of laughter—not sadness or grief,
but just the weather, unbroken, of it all.

Triptych:

Nathan Gold, Maria, *On the Waterfront*

Nathan Gold

9/14/01. So, Sollie, here I am again, an old man,
zeyde, now. You're gone ten years, but it's your birthday
and I'm standing here as always on Brooklyn Bridge
and staring at that skyline, writing it all down.
The longest journey in this country, Uncle Mike
would say, *stretches from the Lower East Side to
the Upper East,* and weekends you would see them there,
the rich, the big shots, strolling to the Met, say,
or Guggenheim to see the Rembrandts or Chagalls,
gold flecks of light drifting down through leafy branches
to settle on the shoulders of their silk, tailored suits.
So I'm halfway: a three-room near the Chelsea, not bad,
considering what might have been. Some years ago
I ran into Reznikoff at Dubrow's on Seventh Ave.
when he was writing *Holocaust,* and he blurts out,
*Eichmann said his entire life was founded on
one moral principle: Kant's categorical imperative,
later modified for the "small man's household use."*
My God, can you believe it? Food spewed from his mouth,
his hands were shaking. *Thousands murdered everyday.*
He read Kant and yet . . . ! Language rendered useless.
Thought turned inside out. Rez wrote his poems true to fact
but often with a sense of failure. Three days ago
I knew this sense, words failing, as the towers drowned

in smoke, as the *malach hamoves* spread its wings
across the city. Rabbi Stern, a good man, a holy man,
prayed in its shadow, bewildered as the rest of us.
And so, Crane's poem, *Under thy shadow by the piers*
I waited; Only in darkness is thy shadow clear . . .
but *lend a myth to God?* No, I don't think so. The wings
are spread too wide this time and stain the river gray
the way that Kansas dust storm turned the sky death-gray
when we were boys on our trip out west, hitchhiking,
all that space, all that American space Crane's bridge
embraced, and not just Brooklyn to Manhattan, but coast
to coast, *Vaulting the sea, the prairies' dreaming sod,*
and he should be here now as I am, groping for
the words, the true ones, for a country and a city
like none anywhere whose streets are shrouded gray
(some days, Mike said, near Lublin it came down
like snow, like *snow*), whose skies are ruined with ash.

Maria

Maria Rasputin, b. 1898, Siberia; d. 1977,
Los Angeles, California

They say the fortress has been taken; it is evening,
it is dark, rebelling horseguards just went past with
music. Autos race along Zagrodny without cease; they
are met with shouts of "Hurrah!" Soldiers and workers
shoot into the air, there are few people out, it is noisy and
dark; soldiers roam around in groups, smoke, and shoot
aimlessly. The revolution has taken the form of a military
uprising. . . . Chaos, forces of the century.
                    —The Diaries of Nikolay Punin, 1917

A circus. Circles. Everything comes round, Pyotr.
May I call you Pyotr? I knew so many then.
Look up there, the freeway, cars trunk to tail like
circus elephants. Feed them or they'll trample you.
I know. Ringling Brothers. I trained animals,
but lions mostly. Yes. Almost killed once, a bear
in Indiana. Russia, Budapest. And Paris,
where I danced in cabarets, then New York, later
Florida, now L.A. A riveter in Long Beach,
but too old now, I babysit for the bourgeois rich,
and when they ask for my credentials, I say,

I babysat the daughters of the Czar of Russia.
That shuts them up. You're too polite, of course, to ask
about my father. "Mad Monk," indeed. I don't know,
the women, that crazy cult. And God knows I'm no saint
myself. But all past. Long time. Vodka under the bridge.
He was my father, and he loved me. History
judges him, nothing I can do. Listen: *history*
is a mess, just one damned thing and then another.
Believe me, I know. *I was there.* The door of history
closes, opens. It opened, I went through. Czar,
Czarina, children, gone. Varya, Mitia, gone.
All gone. And I survive. Two husbands, five countries,
two wars, and look, I'm here talking to Blake scholar,
yes? Blake, the one with visions, angels, yes? You come
to study in the mansion of the Railroad King.
The bourgeois rich. My father had a vision and told
Czar Nicholas, *Don't go to war. It's Serbia,*
not our affair. Everything comes round. Pyotr,
you say your father fought in World War Two. The mess
of history being what it is, does it not amaze you,
but for a little man named Wilhelm with a withered arm,
a tiny brain, and a Germany to play with,
there might not have been a First World War, a vengeful peace,
an Adolf, another war, and you, like thousands more,
without a father? *They murdered mine.* Mad, maybe,
but he told him twice. Or that if the Archduke's idiot
driver had turned right instead of left, then no
assassination, no *Great War*, and decades later,
no absent fathers. Maybe. *But he had a vision!*

He knew! History is a mess: whatever we do now,
a hundred years from now they're burying the victims.
Bozhe moi. In Paris, just before I left, there was
a man named Kojève whose idea was *the end
of history,* and *desire,* the little engine running it.
Intellectuals in the cabarets would speak of it.
(What did I know? Like you, I come from peasants.
I just listened.) And in Ringling Brothers, something
called a *freak show,* was a little girl named Frieda Pushnik
with only half a body. Intelligent, so brave,
a soul, no arms to push against the world, no legs
to run away from it. Well, I'm a freak of history,
I thought. She can do it, so can I. And so I did.
So, Pyotr, look again. Up there. The freeway, trunk
to tail like circus elephants. And who will feed them?
Who will they trample to get more? There's your *desire,*
your *want,* and trust me, it is endless. But the end
of history? Oh no, Pyotr. It's only just begun.

On the Waterfront

know thyself

Flashlight in hand, I stand just inside the door
in my starched white shirt, red jacket nailed shut
by six gold buttons, and a plastic black bowtie,
a sort of smaller movie screen reflecting back
the larger one. *Is that really you?* says Mrs. Pierce,
my Latin teacher, as I lead her to her seat
between the Neiderlands, our neighbors, and Mickey Breen,
who owns the liquor store. Walking back, I see
their faces bright and childlike in the mirrored glare
of a tragic winter New York sky. I know them all,
these small-town worried faces, these natives of the known,
the real, a highway and brown fields, and New York
is a foreign land—the waterfront, unions, priests,
the tugboat's moan—exotic as Siam or Casablanca.
I have seen this movie seven times, memorized the lines:
Edie, raised by nuns, pleading—praying, really—
Isn't everybody a part of everybody else?
and Terry, angry, stunned with guilt, *Quit worrying
about the truth. Worry about yourself,* while I,
in this one-movie Kansas town where everyone
is a part of everybody else, am waiting darkly
for a self to worry over, a name, a place,

New York, on 52nd Street between the Five Spot
and Jimmy Ryan's where bebop and blue neon lights
would fill my room and I would wear a porkpie hat
and play tenor saxophone like Lester Young, but now,
however, I am lost, and Edie, too, and Charlie,
Father Barry, Pop, even Terry because he worried
more about the truth than he did about himself,
and I scan the little mounds of bodies now lost even
to themselves as the movie rushes to its end,
car lights winging down an alley, quick shadows
fluttering across this East River of familiar faces
like storm clouds cluttering a wheat field or geese
in autumn plowing through the sun, that honking,
that moan of a boat in fog. I walk outside
to cop a smoke, *I could have been a contender,*
I could have been somebody instead of . . . who I am,
and look across the street at the Army-Navy store
where we would try on gas masks, and Elmer Fox
would let us hold the Purple Hearts, but it's over now,
and they are leaving, *Goodnight, Mr. Neiderland,*
Goodnight, Mrs. Neiderland, Goodnight, Mick, Goodnight,
Mrs. Pierce, as she, a woman who has lived alone
for forty years and for two of those has suffered through
my botched translations from the Latin tongue, smiles,
Nosce te ipsum, and I have no idea what she means.

Notes

"Usher," pages 27–32: Known as the "master builder," Robert Moses, Arterial Coordinator of New York City, enjoyed unprecedented power as an urban designer, radically altering the landscape and urban sociology of the city through his mammoth freeway projects, including the Cross Bronx Expressway, the construction of which (from 1948 to 1963) destroyed numerous blue-collar and middle-class neighborhoods, many of them predominantly Jewish. Arguably two of the four or five most important Protestant theologians of the twentieth century, Paul Tillich and Reinhold Niebuhr taught at Union Theological Seminary in Manhattan during the 1950s. Tillich's most widely read works for a popular audience were *The Courage to Be* and *Dynamics of Faith*. "The Heraclitean way" refers to the statement in the fragments of Heraclitus that "the path up and down is one and the same." In his reference to the Isenheim Altarpiece in Colmar, France, at the Musée d'Unterlínden, Nathan is thinking of the right side panel depicting Christ risen from the tomb.

"Hart Crane in Havana": see "Key" on pages 37–39.

"The Cottonwood Lounge," pages 43–44: George Cantor, German mathematician (1845–1918), created set theory as well as the very controversial theory of transfinite numbers. He died in a mental institution.

"Wittgenstein, Dying," pages 47–48: "Trakl" refers, of course, to Georg Trakl, the Austrian poet, whom Wittgenstein admired and to whom he gave a small portion of his inheritance though he confessed himself unable fully to understand Trakl's poems. Although World War I was "the nightmare of the earth" for all involved (and through a long line of historical connections continues to be), it was especially so for Trakl, who died from a cocaine overdose in 1914. Wittgenstein's *On Certainty* was written partially in response to G. E. Moore's argument against skepticism, which begins with Moore holding up one hand, pointing to it with the other, and saying, "This is one hand." "Paul" is Paul Wittgenstein, Ludwig's brother, a concert pianist who lost his right arm in World War One but continued performing, commissioning works for the left hand from such composers as Ravel, Strauss, and Britten.

"Gödel," pages 55–56: Kurt Gödel, Czech-born American mathematician and philosopher, who worked with Einstein at the Princeton Institute for Advanced Study, was best known for his incompleteness theorem. Nowhere did Gödel say that "no life contains its own clear validation"; that is solely Ira Campbell's inference. "Lansky" refers to Meyer Lansky, the legendary American mobster known especially for his financial shrewdness.

"Five Prose Poems from the Journals of Roy Eldridge Garcia," pages 59–67: Roy Eldridge Garcia appears in "The Welder, Visited by the Angel of Mercy," *The Art of the Lathe* (Alice James Books, 1998) and "The Blue Buick," *Early Occult Memory Systems of the Lower Midwest* (W. W. Norton, 2002).

"The Beauty of Abandoned Towns," pages 70–75: My loose, colloquial translation of the Latin epigraph is, "Work defeated everything, back-breaking work, and the grinding need of hard times." *The Appeal to Reason*, edited by J. A. Wayland and later by Emanuel Julius, had the largest circulation of any socialist newspaper in the world before World War I.

"The Church of the New Jerusalem, Pawnee Rock, Kansas," pages 87–89: For a brief time the poet William Blake and his wife, Catherine, were members of the Swedenborgian Church of the New Jerusalem in London. Blake later satirized some of the ideas of Swedenborg—scientist/engineer, theologian, and spiritual visionary—in *The Marriage of Heaven and Hell*.

"Nathan Gold," pages 111–12: The American Objectivist poet, Charles Reznikoff, published his long poem, *Holocaust,* in 1975. Material for the poem was based upon transcriptions of court proceedings of the Nuremburg trial and the Eichmann trial. Eichmann's "use" of Kant is discussed at length in Hannah Arendt's *Eichmann in Jerusalem*. The *malach hamoves* is the Hebrew angel of death. Hart Crane's lines quoted here are from the final two stanzas of "To Brooklyn Bridge":

> *Under thy shadow by the piers I waited;*
> *Only in darkness is thy shadow clear.*
> *The City's fiery parcels all undone,*
> *Already snow submerges an iron year . . .*

O Sleepless as the river under thee,
Vaulting the sea, the prairies' dreaming sod,
Unto us lowliest sometime sweep, descend
And of the curveship lend a myth to God.

"Maria," pages 113–15: Maria Rasputin, oldest daughter of the infamous Grigori Rasputin, is not to be confused with the Maria of "Cendrars," on page 61. "The mansion of the Railroad King" refers to the Huntington Library in Pasadena, California, a center for research on the poet William Blake. Alexandre Kojève (1902–1968) was a French philosopher born in Russia who exerted an immense influence on both European and American intellectuals, including the political philospher Leo Strauss; Allan Bloom (Strauss's student who later studied with Kojève); Bloom's student, Francis Fukuyama; and many others in both academic and political life. Fukuyama's book, *The End of History and the Last Man,* incorporated ideas and themes from Kojève.